THIS MUSIC LESSON
PRACTICE RECORD
BELONGS TO:

_____

_____

NOTES:

LESSON DATE:

ASSIGNMENTS

WARM UP
EXERCISES: _____
_____
_____

BOOK	PAGE	TITLE	FOCUS ON

TEACHER COMMENTS:
_____
_____
_____
_____

PRACTICE LOG

GOAL: _____ MINUTES PER DAY

S	M	T	W	TH	F	S
☐	☐	☐	☐	☐	☐	☐

STUDENT COMMENTS / QUESTIONS:
_____
_____
_____
_____

NOTES:

LESSON DATE:

ASSIGNMENTS

WARM UP
EXERCISES: _____
_____
_____

BOOK	PAGE	TITLE	FOCUS ON

TEACHER COMMENTS:
_____
_____
_____

PRACTICE LOG

GOAL: _____ MINUTES PER DAY

S	M	T	W	TH	F	S
☐	☐	☐	☐	☐	☐	☐

STUDENT COMMENTS / QUESTIONS:
_____
_____
_____

NOTES:

LESSON DATE:

ASSIGNMENTS

WARM UP
EXERCISES: _____
_____
_____

BOOK	PAGE	TITLE	FOCUS ON

TEACHER COMMENTS:

_____
_____
_____
_____

PRACTICE LOG

GOAL: _____ MINUTES PER DAY

S	M	T	W	TH	F	S
☐	☐	☐	☐	☐	☐	☐

STUDENT COMMENTS / QUESTIONS:

_____
_____
_____
_____

NOTES:

LESSON DATE:

ASSIGNMENTS

WARM UP
EXERCISES: _____
_____
_____

BOOK	PAGE	TITLE	FOCUS ON

TEACHER COMMENTS:

_____
_____
_____
_____

PRACTICE LOG

GOAL: _____ MINUTES PER DAY

S	M	T	W	TH	F	S
☐	☐	☐	☐	☐	☐	☐

STUDENT COMMENTS / QUESTIONS:

_____
_____
_____
_____

NOTES:

LESSON DATE:

ASSIGNMENTS

WARM UP
EXERCISES: _____
_____
_____

BOOK	PAGE	TITLE	FOCUS ON

TEACHER COMMENTS:
_____
_____
_____

PRACTICE LOG

GOAL: _____ MINUTES PER DAY

S	M	T	W	TH	F	S

STUDENT COMMENTS / QUESTIONS:
_____
_____
_____
_____

NOTES:

LESSON DATE:

ASSIGNMENTS

WARM UP
EXERCISES: _____
_____
_____

BOOK	PAGE	TITLE	FOCUS ON

TEACHER COMMENTS:

_____
_____
_____
_____

PRACTICE LOG

GOAL: _____ MINUTES PER DAY

S	M	T	W	TH	F	S
☐	☐	☐	☐	☐	☐	☐

STUDENT COMMENTS / QUESTIONS:

_____
_____
_____
_____

NOTES:

LESSON DATE:

ASSIGNMENTS

WARM UP
EXERCISES: _____
_____

BOOK	PAGE	TITLE	FOCUS ON

TEACHER COMMENTS:

_____

_____

_____

PRACTICE LOG

GOAL: _____ MINUTES PER DAY

S	M	T	W	TH	F	S

STUDENT COMMENTS / QUESTIONS:

_____

_____

_____

NOTES:

LESSON DATE:

ASSIGNMENTS

WARM UP
EXERCISES: _____

BOOK	PAGE	TITLE	FOCUS ON

TEACHER COMMENTS:

_____

_____

_____

PRACTICE LOG

GOAL: _____ MINUTES PER DAY

S	M	T	W	TH	F	S

STUDENT COMMENTS / QUESTIONS:

_____

_____

_____

NOTES:

LESSON DATE:

ASSIGNMENTS

WARM UP
EXERCISES: _____
_____
_____

BOOK	PAGE	TITLE	FOCUS ON

TEACHER COMMENTS:
_____
_____
_____
_____

PRACTICE LOG

GOAL: _____ MINUTES PER DAY

S	M	T	W	TH	F	S

STUDENT COMMENTS / QUESTIONS:
_____
_____
_____
_____

NOTES:

LESSON DATE:

ASSIGNMENTS

WARM UP
EXERCISES: _____
_____

BOOK	PAGE	TITLE	FOCUS ON

TEACHER COMMENTS:

_____
_____
_____

PRACTICE LOG

GOAL: _____ MINUTES PER DAY

S	M	T	W	TH	F	S

STUDENT COMMENTS / QUESTIONS:

_____
_____
_____
_____

NOTES:

LESSON DATE:

ASSIGNMENTS

WARM UP
EXERCISES: _____
_____

BOOK	PAGE	TITLE	FOCUS ON

TEACHER COMMENTS:
_____
_____
_____

PRACTICE LOG

GOAL: _____ MINUTES PER DAY

S	M	T	W	TH	F	S
☐	☐	☐	☐	☐	☐	☐

STUDENT COMMENTS / QUESTIONS:
_____
_____
_____

NOTES:

LESSON DATE:

ASSIGNMENTS

WARM UP
EXERCISES: _____

BOOK	PAGE	TITLE	FOCUS ON

TEACHER COMMENTS:

PRACTICE LOG

GOAL: _____ MINUTES PER DAY

S	M	T	W	TH	F	S

STUDENT COMMENTS / QUESTIONS:

NOTES:

LESSON DATE:

ASSIGNMENTS

WARM UP
EXERCISES: _____

BOOK	PAGE	TITLE	FOCUS ON

TEACHER COMMENTS:

_____
_____
_____

PRACTICE LOG

GOAL: _____ MINUTES PER DAY

S	M	T	W	TH	F	S

STUDENT COMMENTS / QUESTIONS:

_____
_____
_____
_____

NOTES:

LESSON DATE:

ASSIGNMENTS

WARM UP
EXERCISES: _____
_____
_____

BOOK	PAGE	TITLE	FOCUS ON

TEACHER COMMENTS:

_____

_____

_____

PRACTICE LOG

GOAL: _____ MINUTES PER DAY

S	M	T	W	TH	F	S
☐	☐	☐	☐	☐	☐	☐

STUDENT COMMENTS / QUESTIONS:

_____

_____

_____

NOTES:

LESSON DATE:

ASSIGNMENTS

WARM UP
EXERCISES: _____
_____
_____

BOOK	PAGE	TITLE	FOCUS ON

TEACHER COMMENTS:
_____
_____
_____

PRACTICE LOG

GOAL: _____ MINUTES PER DAY

S	M	T	W	TH	F	S

STUDENT COMMENTS / QUESTIONS:
_____
_____
_____
_____

NOTES:

LESSON DATE:

ASSIGNMENTS

WARM UP
EXERCISES: _____
_____
_____

BOOK	PAGE	TITLE	FOCUS ON

TEACHER COMMENTS:
_____
_____
_____

PRACTICE LOG

GOAL: _____ MINUTES PER DAY

S	M	T	W	TH	F	S
☐	☐	☐	☐	☐	☐	☐

STUDENT COMMENTS / QUESTIONS:
_____
_____
_____

NOTES:

LESSON DATE:

ASSIGNMENTS

WARM UP
EXERCISES: _____
_____

BOOK	PAGE	TITLE	FOCUS ON

TEACHER COMMENTS:
_____
_____
_____
_____

PRACTICE LOG

GOAL: _____ MINUTES PER DAY

S	M	T	W	TH	F	S
☐	☐	☐	☐	☐	☐	☐

STUDENT COMMENTS / QUESTIONS:
_____
_____
_____
_____

NOTES:

LESSON DATE:

ASSIGNMENTS

WARM UP
EXERCISES: _____
_____

BOOK	PAGE	TITLE	FOCUS ON

TEACHER COMMENTS:

_____
_____
_____

PRACTICE LOG

GOAL: _____ MINUTES PER DAY

S	M	T	W	TH	F	S
☐	☐	☐	☐	☐	☐	☐

STUDENT COMMENTS / QUESTIONS:

_____
_____
_____

NOTES:

LESSON DATE:

ASSIGNMENTS

WARM UP
EXERCISES: _____

BOOK	PAGE	TITLE	FOCUS ON

TEACHER COMMENTS:

_____
_____
_____

PRACTICE LOG

GOAL: _____ MINUTES PER DAY

S	M	T	W	TH	F	S
☐	☐	☐	☐	☐	☐	☐

STUDENT COMMENTS / QUESTIONS:

_____
_____
_____

NOTES:

LESSON DATE:

ASSIGNMENTS

WARM UP
EXERCISES: _____
_____
_____

BOOK	PAGE	TITLE	FOCUS ON

TEACHER COMMENTS:

_____
_____
_____

PRACTICE LOG

GOAL: _____ MINUTES PER DAY

S	M	T	W	TH	F	S

STUDENT COMMENTS / QUESTIONS:

_____
_____
_____
_____

LESSON DATE:

ASSIGNMENTS

WARM UP
EXERCISES: _____
_____
_____

BOOK	PAGE	TITLE	FOCUS ON

TEACHER COMMENTS:

_____
_____
_____
_____

PRACTICE LOG

GOAL: _____ MINUTES PER DAY

S	M	T	W	TH	F	S
☐	☐	☐	☐	☐	☐	☐

STUDENT COMMENTS / QUESTIONS:

_____
_____
_____
_____

NOTES:

LESSON DATE:

ASSIGNMENTS

WARM UP
EXERCISES: _____
_____
_____

BOOK	PAGE	TITLE	FOCUS ON

TEACHER COMMENTS:
_____
_____
_____

PRACTICE LOG

GOAL: _____ MINUTES PER DAY

S	M	T	W	TH	F	S
☐	☐	☐	☐	☐	☐	☐

STUDENT COMMENTS / QUESTIONS:
_____
_____
_____

NOTES:

LESSON DATE:

ASSIGNMENTS

WARM UP
EXERCISES: _____
_____
_____

BOOK	PAGE	TITLE	FOCUS ON

TEACHER COMMENTS:
_____
_____
_____
_____

PRACTICE LOG

GOAL: _____ MINUTES PER DAY

S	M	T	W	TH	F	S
☐	☐	☐	☐	☐	☐	☐

STUDENT COMMENTS / QUESTIONS:
_____
_____
_____
_____

NOTES:

LESSON DATE:

ASSIGNMENTS

WARM UP
EXERCISES: _____
_____
_____

BOOK	PAGE	TITLE	FOCUS ON

TEACHER COMMENTS:

_____
_____
_____

PRACTICE LOG

GOAL: _____ MINUTES PER DAY

S	M	T	W	TH	F	S
☐	☐	☐	☐	☐	☐	☐

STUDENT COMMENTS / QUESTIONS:

_____
_____
_____
_____

NOTES:

LESSON DATE:

ASSIGNMENTS

WARM UP
EXERCISES: _____
_____

BOOK	PAGE	TITLE	FOCUS ON

TEACHER COMMENTS:
_____
_____
_____

PRACTICE LOG

GOAL: _____ MINUTES PER DAY

S	M	T	W	TH	F	S

STUDENT COMMENTS / QUESTIONS:
_____
_____
_____
_____

NOTES:

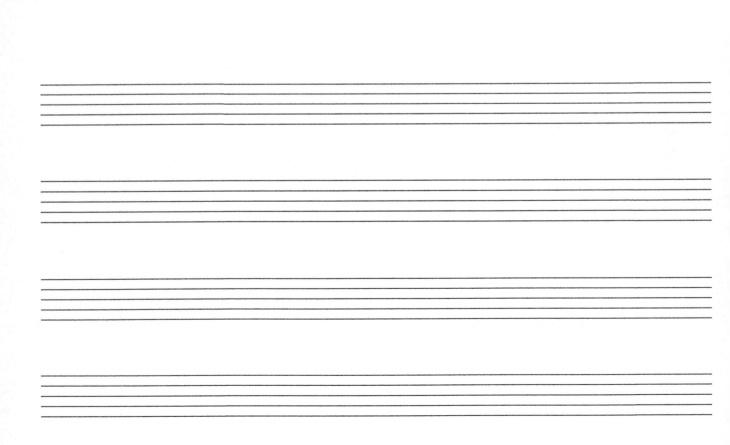

LESSON DATE:

ASSIGNMENTS

WARM UP
EXERCISES: _____
_____
_____

BOOK	PAGE	TITLE	FOCUS ON

TEACHER COMMENTS:
_____
_____
_____

PRACTICE LOG

GOAL: _____ MINUTES PER DAY

S	M	T	W	TH	F	S
☐	☐	☐	☐	☐	☐	☐

STUDENT COMMENTS / QUESTIONS:
_____
_____
_____
_____

NOTES:

LESSON DATE:

ASSIGNMENTS

WARM UP
EXERCISES: _____
_____

BOOK	PAGE	TITLE	FOCUS ON

TEACHER COMMENTS:
_____
_____
_____

PRACTICE LOG

GOAL: _____ MINUTES PER DAY

S	M	T	W	TH	F	S
☐	☐	☐	☐	☐	☐	☐

STUDENT COMMENTS / QUESTIONS:
_____
_____
_____
_____

NOTES:

LESSON DATE:

ASSIGNMENTS

WARM UP
EXERCISES: _____
_____
_____

BOOK	PAGE	TITLE	FOCUS ON

TEACHER COMMENTS:
_____
_____
_____

PRACTICE LOG

GOAL: _____ MINUTES PER DAY

S	M	T	W	TH	F	S

STUDENT COMMENTS / QUESTIONS:
_____
_____
_____
_____

LESSON DATE:

ASSIGNMENTS

WARM UP
EXERCISES: _____
_____

BOOK	PAGE	TITLE	FOCUS ON

TEACHER COMMENTS:
_____
_____
_____

PRACTICE LOG

GOAL: _____ MINUTES PER DAY

S	M	T	W	TH	F	S

STUDENT COMMENTS / QUESTIONS:
_____
_____
_____

NOTES:

LESSON DATE:

ASSIGNMENTS

WARM UP
EXERCISES: _____
_____

BOOK	PAGE	TITLE	FOCUS ON

TEACHER COMMENTS:

_____
_____
_____

PRACTICE LOG

GOAL: _____ MINUTES PER DAY

S	M	T	W	TH	F	S

STUDENT COMMENTS / QUESTIONS:

_____
_____
_____
_____

NOTES:

LESSON DATE:

ASSIGNMENTS

WARM UP
EXERCISES: _____
_____
_____

BOOK	PAGE	TITLE	FOCUS ON

TEACHER COMMENTS:

_____
_____
_____

PRACTICE LOG

GOAL: _____ MINUTES PER DAY

S	M	T	W	TH	F	S

STUDENT COMMENTS / QUESTIONS:

_____
_____
_____
_____

NOTES:

LESSON DATE:

ASSIGNMENTS

WARM UP
EXERCISES: _____
_____
_____

BOOK	PAGE	TITLE	FOCUS ON

TEACHER COMMENTS:
_____
_____
_____

PRACTICE LOG

GOAL: _____ MINUTES PER DAY

S	M	T	W	TH	F	S

STUDENT COMMENTS / QUESTIONS:
_____
_____
_____
_____

NOTES:

LESSON DATE:

ASSIGNMENTS

WARM UP
EXERCISES: _____
_____

BOOK	PAGE	TITLE	FOCUS ON

TEACHER COMMENTS:
_____
_____
_____

PRACTICE LOG

GOAL: _____ MINUTES PER DAY

S	M	T	W	TH	F	S
☐	☐	☐	☐	☐	☐	☐

STUDENT COMMENTS / QUESTIONS:
_____
_____
_____
_____

NOTES:

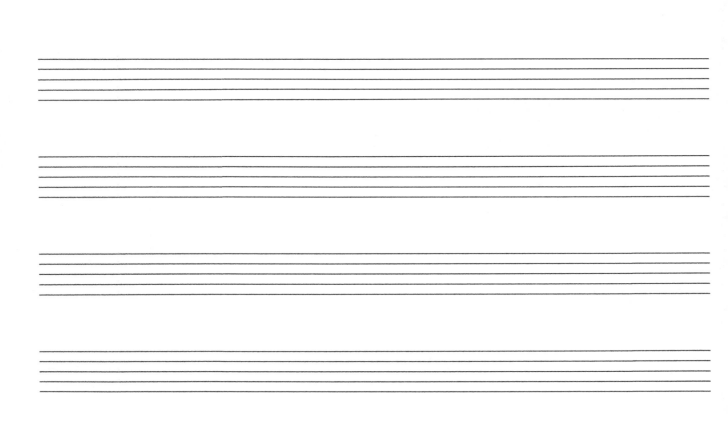

LESSON DATE:

ASSIGNMENTS

WARM UP
EXERCISES: _____
_____
_____

BOOK	PAGE	TITLE	FOCUS ON

TEACHER COMMENTS:
_____
_____
_____

PRACTICE LOG

GOAL: _____ MINUTES PER DAY

S	M	T	W	TH	F	S
☐	☐	☐	☐	☐	☐	☐

STUDENT COMMENTS / QUESTIONS:
_____
_____
_____
_____

NOTES:

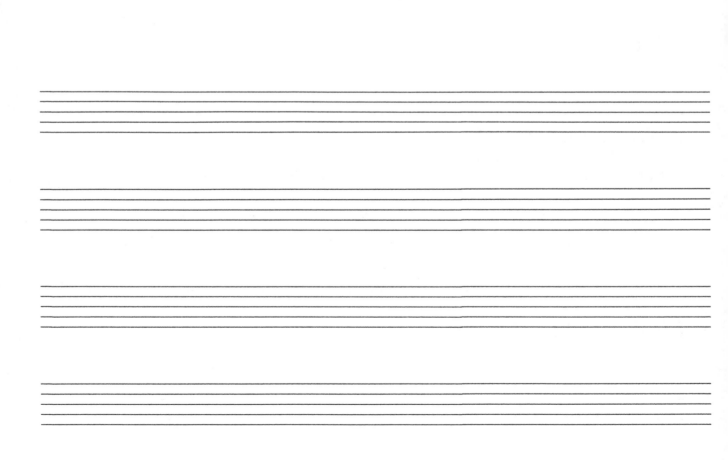

LESSON DATE:

ASSIGNMENTS

WARM UP
EXERCISES: _____
_____

BOOK	PAGE	TITLE	FOCUS ON

TEACHER COMMENTS:

_____
_____
_____

PRACTICE LOG

GOAL: _____ MINUTES PER DAY

S	M	T	W	TH	F	S
☐	☐	☐	☐	☐	☐	☐

STUDENT COMMENTS / QUESTIONS:

_____
_____
_____
_____

NOTES:

LESSON DATE:

ASSIGNMENTS

WARM UP
EXERCISES: _____
_____
_____

BOOK	PAGE	TITLE	FOCUS ON

TEACHER COMMENTS:
_____
_____
_____

PRACTICE LOG

GOAL: _____ MINUTES PER DAY

S	M	T	W	TH	F	S

STUDENT COMMENTS / QUESTIONS:
_____
_____
_____
_____

NOTES:

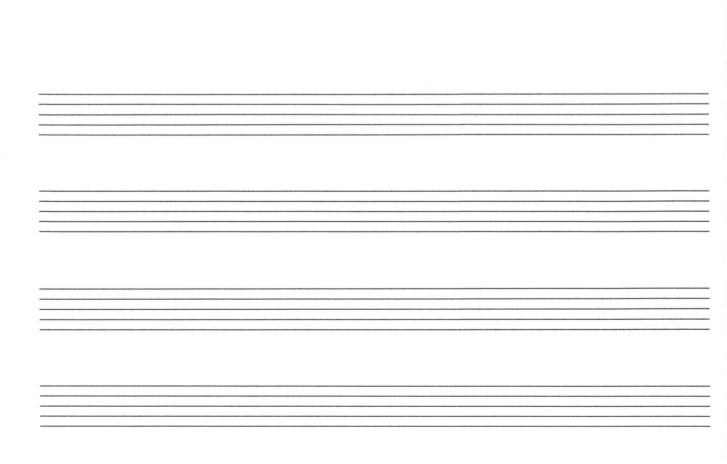

LESSON DATE:

ASSIGNMENTS

WARM UP
EXERCISES: _____
_____

BOOK	PAGE	TITLE	FOCUS ON

TEACHER COMMENTS:
_____
_____
_____

PRACTICE LOG

GOAL: _____ MINUTES PER DAY

S	M	T	W	TH	F	S

STUDENT COMMENTS / QUESTIONS:
_____
_____
_____
_____

NOTES:

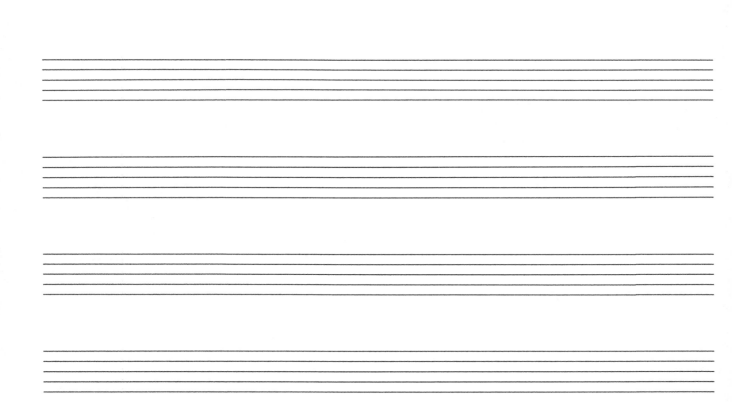

LESSON DATE:

ASSIGNMENTS

WARM UP
EXERCISES: _____
_____

BOOK	PAGE	TITLE	FOCUS ON

TEACHER COMMENTS:

_____
_____
_____

PRACTICE LOG

GOAL: _____ MINUTES PER DAY

S	M	T	W	TH	F	S

STUDENT COMMENTS / QUESTIONS:

_____
_____
_____

NOTES:

LESSON DATE:

ASSIGNMENTS

WARM UP
EXERCISES: _____
_____

BOOK	PAGE	TITLE	FOCUS ON

TEACHER COMMENTS:
_____
_____
_____

PRACTICE LOG

GOAL: _____ MINUTES PER DAY

S	M	T	W	TH	F	S
☐	☐	☐	☐	☐	☐	☐

STUDENT COMMENTS / QUESTIONS:
_____
_____
_____

NOTES:

LESSON DATE:

ASSIGNMENTS

WARM UP
EXERCISES: _____
_____

BOOK	PAGE	TITLE	FOCUS ON	

TEACHER COMMENTS:
_____
_____
_____

PRACTICE LOG

GOAL: _____ MINUTES PER DAY

S	M	T	W	TH	F	S
☐	☐	☐	☐	☐	☐	☐

STUDENT COMMENTS / QUESTIONS:
_____
_____
_____

NOTES:

LESSON DATE:

ASSIGNMENTS

WARM UP
EXERCISES: _____
_____
_____

BOOK	PAGE	TITLE	FOCUS ON

TEACHER COMMENTS:

_____
_____
_____

PRACTICE LOG

GOAL: _____ MINUTES PER DAY

S	M	T	W	TH	F	S
☐	☐	☐	☐	☐	☐	☐

STUDENT COMMENTS / QUESTIONS:

_____
_____
_____
_____

NOTES:

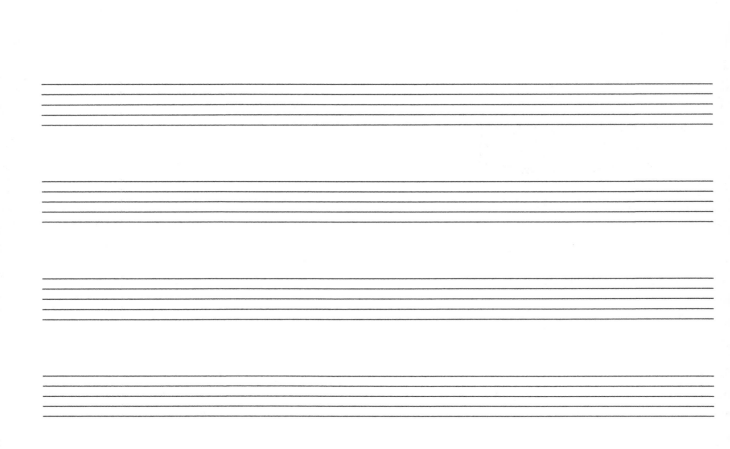

LESSON DATE:

ASSIGNMENTS

WARM UP
EXERCISES: _____
_____

BOOK	PAGE	TITLE	FOCUS ON

TEACHER COMMENTS:

_____
_____
_____

PRACTICE LOG

GOAL: _____ MINUTES PER DAY

S	M	T	W	TH	F	S
☐	☐	☐	☐	☐	☐	☐

STUDENT COMMENTS / QUESTIONS:

_____
_____
_____
_____

NOTES:

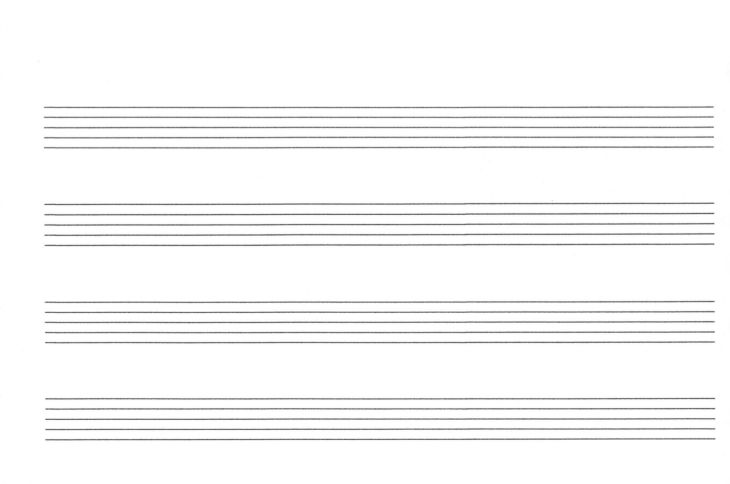

LESSON DATE:

ASSIGNMENTS

WARM UP
EXERCISES: _____
_____
_____

BOOK	PAGE	TITLE	FOCUS ON

TEACHER COMMENTS:
_____
_____
_____

PRACTICE LOG

GOAL: _____ MINUTES PER DAY

S	M	T	W	TH	F	S

STUDENT COMMENTS / QUESTIONS:
_____
_____
_____

NOTES:

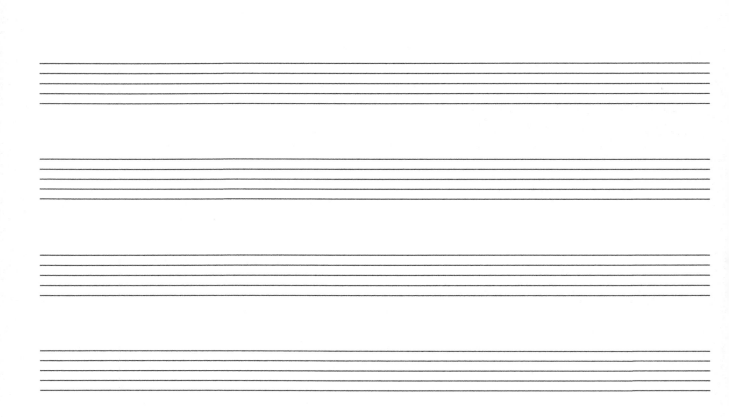

LESSON DATE:

ASSIGNMENTS

WARM UP
EXERCISES: _____
_____
_____

BOOK	PAGE	TITLE	FOCUS ON

TEACHER COMMENTS:
_____
_____
_____

PRACTICE LOG

GOAL: _____ MINUTES PER DAY

S	M	T	W	TH	F	S
☐	☐	☐	☐	☐	☐	☐

STUDENT COMMENTS / QUESTIONS:
_____
_____
_____

NOTES:

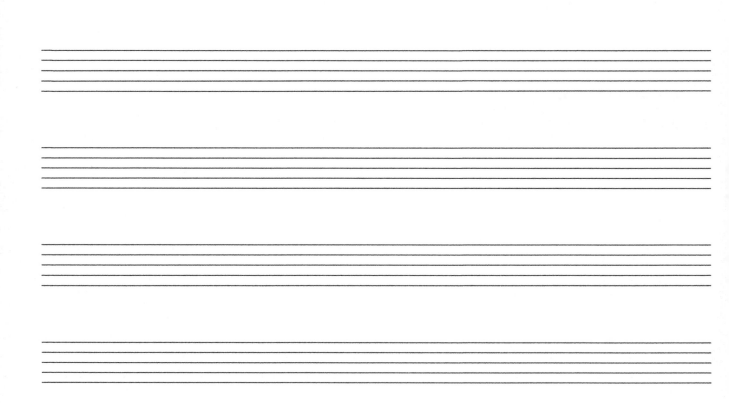

LESSON DATE:

ASSIGNMENTS

WARM UP
EXERCISES: _____
_____

BOOK	PAGE	TITLE	FOCUS ON

TEACHER COMMENTS:

_____
_____
_____

PRACTICE LOG

GOAL: _____ MINUTES PER DAY

S	M	T	W	TH	F	S

STUDENT COMMENTS / QUESTIONS:

_____
_____
_____
_____

NOTES:

LESSON DATE:

ASSIGNMENTS

WARM UP
EXERCISES: _____
_____
_____

BOOK	PAGE	TITLE	FOCUS ON

TEACHER COMMENTS:
_____
_____
_____

PRACTICE LOG

GOAL: _____ MINUTES PER DAY

S	M	T	W	TH	F	S

STUDENT COMMENTS / QUESTIONS:
_____
_____
_____
_____

NOTES:

LESSON DATE:

ASSIGNMENTS

WARM UP
EXERCISES: _____
_____

BOOK	PAGE	TITLE	FOCUS ON

TEACHER COMMENTS:
_____
_____
_____

PRACTICE LOG

GOAL: _____ MINUTES PER DAY

S	M	T	W	TH	F	S
☐	☐	☐	☐	☐	☐	☐

STUDENT COMMENTS / QUESTIONS:
_____
_____
_____
_____

NOTES:

LESSON DATE:

ASSIGNMENTS

WARM UP
EXERCISES: _____
_____
_____

BOOK	PAGE	TITLE	FOCUS ON

TEACHER COMMENTS:
_____
_____
_____

PRACTICE LOG

GOAL: _____ MINUTES PER DAY

S	M	T	W	TH	F	S
☐	☐	☐	☐	☐	☐	☐

STUDENT COMMENTS / QUESTIONS:
_____
_____
_____
_____

NOTES:

LESSON DATE:

ASSIGNMENTS

WARM UP
EXERCISES: _____
_____

BOOK	PAGE	TITLE	FOCUS ON

TEACHER COMMENTS:

_____
_____
_____

PRACTICE LOG

GOAL: _____ MINUTES PER DAY

S	M	T	W	TH	F	S

STUDENT COMMENTS / QUESTIONS:

_____
_____
_____
_____

NOTES:

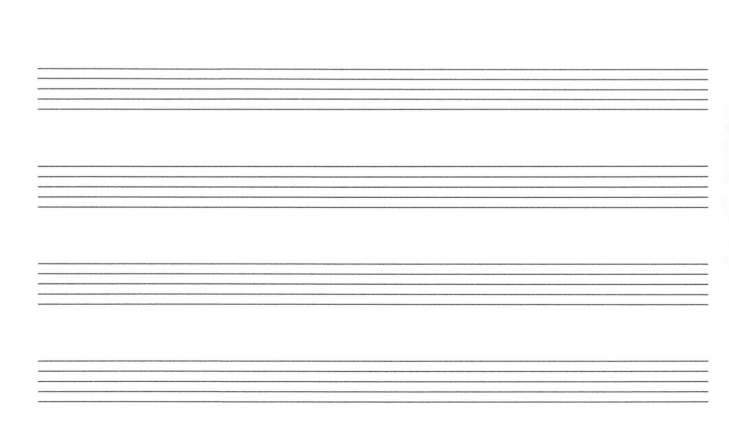

LESSON DATE:

ASSIGNMENTS

WARM UP
EXERCISES: _____
_____

BOOK	PAGE	TITLE	FOCUS ON	

TEACHER COMMENTS:

_____

_____

_____

PRACTICE LOG

GOAL: _____ MINUTES PER DAY

S	M	T	W	TH	F	S
☐	☐	☐	☐	☐	☐	☐

STUDENT COMMENTS / QUESTIONS:

_____

_____

_____

NOTES:

LESSON DATE:

ASSIGNMENTS

WARM UP
EXERCISES: _____
_____

BOOK	PAGE	TITLE	FOCUS ON

TEACHER COMMENTS:
_____
_____
_____

PRACTICE LOG

GOAL: _____ MINUTES PER DAY

S	M	T	W	TH	F	S
☐	☐	☐	☐	☐	☐	☐

STUDENT COMMENTS / QUESTIONS:
_____
_____
_____
_____

NOTES:

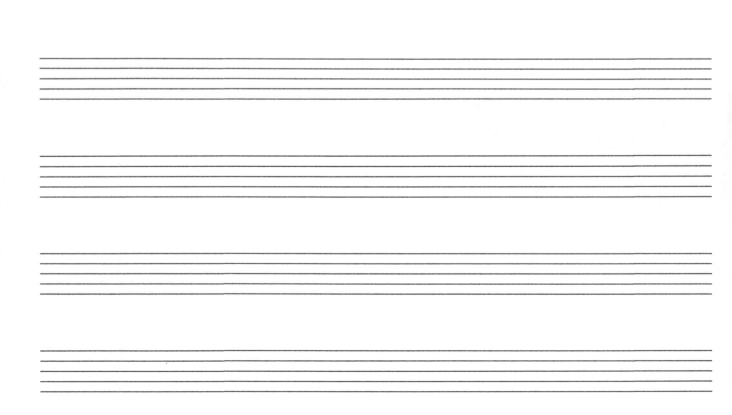

LESSON DATE:

ASSIGNMENTS

WARM UP
EXERCISES: _____
_____

BOOK	PAGE	TITLE	FOCUS ON

TEACHER COMMENTS:

_____
_____
_____

PRACTICE LOG

GOAL: _____ MINUTES PER DAY

S	M	T	W	TH	F	S
☐	☐	☐	☐	☐	☐	☐

STUDENT COMMENTS / QUESTIONS:

_____
_____
_____
_____

PIECES COMPLETED THIS YEAR:

_____   _____
_____   _____
_____   _____
_____   _____
_____   _____
_____   _____
_____   _____
_____   _____
_____   _____
_____   _____
_____   _____
_____   _____
_____   _____
_____   _____
_____   _____
_____   _____

PIECES COMPLETED THIS YEAR:

_____ _____
_____ _____
_____ _____
_____ _____
_____ _____
_____ _____
_____ _____
_____ _____
_____ _____
_____ _____
_____ _____
_____ _____
_____ _____
_____ _____
_____ _____
_____ _____
_____ _____

Made in the USA
Coppell, TX
24 January 2023

11636950R00063